Introduction

We're all born with masculine and feminine energy, and the equal balance of the two is our authentic core where we are our best selves. Masculine energy is the yang, the sun—the logical, ambitious, focused, rational, hyperaggressive, risk-taking, conscious side of yourself. Feminine energy is the yin, the moon—the emotional, nurturing, intuitive, understanding, subconscious side of yourself. But modern life is built around a masculine, and often toxic, form of society—where we focus on dominance, material achievements, and money as definitions of success. This drives us wildly out of balance, and we end up stressed, depressed, anxious, frantic, overwhelmed, apathetic, and lost. Sound familiar?

Let that go.

The pursuit of our goals is driven by our sense of self, our ego—which mediates between our conscious and subconscious (also: masculine and feminine). Our conscious mind can overrule; and our motivations become unbalanced. We then deny aspects of our personalities that don't seem "desirable" or "good" and shove them into our Shadows, the dark side of ourselves where we hide our negative traits deep in our subconscious. But these aspects are actually incredibly important because they are here to teach and guide us. Just like the positive traits you possess proudly in your Light self (the positive, accepted aspects of yourself), these negative traits are beautiful gifts—teaching you where your strengths are and how to wield them. Additionally, suppressing them also suppresses their polarity—just as you can't feel the greatest heights of joy without also knowing the depths of grief. This becomes a problem because many of us eventually reach a point where we feel blocked and numb. We've pushed aspects of ourselves, often traits related to feminine energy, such as emotions and empathy, so far down that we don't know our whole self and all the possibilities of what we're capable of becoming. Our deep unhappiness seeps out of us like a poison contaminating the overall well-being of our community, and creates collective chaos, conflict, and anger. Not only that: we keep attracting these denied aspects over and over in people and experiences until we let ourselves out of our own trap. We project onto others what we dislike in ourselves. This can be when someone else's actions activate a deep self-conscious fear or when others proudly embrace aspects of themselves that you deny for yourself. You can't grow into your greatest potential without owning your whole self and your entire artillery of gifts.

This journal is for working through these blocks, for getting back in touch with your most authentic self and your own divine feminine energy. Through guided exercises inspired by many goddesses and their worship practices, you'll learn to integrate your Light and Shadow selves and find your personal power. You owe it to yourself and everyone around you to focus on doing this work in order to become the bright, brilliant person you were born to be in this life, the fullest and truest version of you. Enlightened, empowered people empower others.

For the sake of this journal, goddess energy and practice is referenced as a universal idea and is based on historical cultural traditions of the divine feminine—and not in any religious practice. Goddess worship is also still a serious religion for many, and while I fully honor and respect those who practice, this journal is not based in that practice. It instead focuses on incorporating the psychological aspect of the divine feminine through metaphysical and cultural exercises to help us grow.

Goddesses represent the divine feminine within all of us, and humans have developed ancient practices for accessing that energy, thereby releasing the feminine intuition locked in our Shadows. Tapping into that energy is the only way we'll be able to get back in balance. The pages that follow will guide you in exercises on releasing your fears, healing your heart, practicing self-care, and sending your goals out into the universe. Some of them will ask you to journal through the process; the writing practice will help break through the initial surface reactions and dive deep down into your subconscious. That's where your personal wisdom lives, where the goddess speaks through you. When your goddess self is embraced, you will be grounded, kind, patient, loving, nurturing, inspired, and passionate. So when your "inner goddess" is referred to in these pages, it's about allowing your emotional side and personal divinity to flow freely.

This journal is all about turning inward and doing the work of accepting both your Light and Shadow selves. It's for owning what is already a part of you, honoring your emotions, and understanding that you are the sum of all these things. The goddess, the bad, and the ugly. This journal is also a place for you to write about your experiences as you live them, and to work through either the lessons or the signs the universe is trying to show you. Look for patterns in what you're experiencing, especially when you're stuck. Find a patron goddess to help you through. And, finally, this is a place for you to record all the things you love and the things you do to honor yourself. When you face the things you fear and respect the things you love, that's embracing your power. Then you'll soon find yourself on the other side. You will be the one who sets you free, the one who fills your heart with gratitude and light.

Get ready to be legendary.

Kuan Yin

LEANING INTO COMPASSION

Kuan Yin, the Chinese goddess of mercy and compassion, is here to guide you through challenging periods in your life that call for more care. Since her specialty is healing and understanding through kindness, invoke her when you're feeling especially beaten down, and when you need to work through difficult situations. Compassion is an incredibly powerful tool for healing—it's giving others or yourself the space you need to do what needs to be done, and to wholly accept the process and emotions in the meantime. This goddess reminds us that to alleviate our suffering, we have to practice self-compassion often. We are often hardest on ourselves.

To invoke Kuan Yin, you may:

Build an altar. Make a sacred space with an image of Kuan Yin, and place a white, light-blue, or yellow candle next to it. You may also use objects—a lotus, a bowl of water with light blue-green crystals such as aquamarine or jade, or willow branches—to symbolize Kuan Yin's presence.

Chanting meditation. Often worshippers of Kuan Yin will simply chant her name over and over as a focal point for their thoughts, allowing her spirit to come over them and fill them with peace and harmony. Light a candle for her at the altar, sit comfortably, and chant her name for ten minutes, allowing the power of the ritual to rise within you.

Walking meditation. Worshipping Kuan Yin and inviting in this divine goddess of mercy can be very simple; some practice repeating her name softly or silently to themselves throughout the day—perhaps during a walk. You may feel her presence physically with you or channeling through you in the form of new ideas when focusing on her name.

Visualization meditation. Sit with your spine straight and close your eyes. Inhale deeply, then exhale. Repeat eight times. Then visualize that you're in nature, coming across a rainbow bridge over brilliant, sparkling water. As you cross the bridge, you find yourself becoming more and more calm. You arrive at Kuan Yin's island of P'u T'o Shan. The goddess is here to greet you, handing you a gorgeous, fragrant flower. You follow her through a lush, tropical island to her pavilion. There, she first washes your feet and then serves you what you need. You are seated facing each other, and she asks what's troubling you. You pour out your heart to her, and she listens intently. She gives you all the patience, love, and attention you need, filling you with support and Light. You feel utterly loved, seen, and heard. Sit with her until you feel whole. Then she'll take you back to the rainbow bridge, and you will embrace her and express your deepest gratitude. The return trip over the rainbow bridge is even faster than you remember, and you come back into your body, feeling lighter and integrating the feelings of patience, love, and compassion into your heart so that you may give it to yourself and to others who may need it.

WRITTEN IN THE STARS

Known as the mother of the endless universe, Hindu goddess Aditi is said to have created all the astrological constellations in the sky. Your sun sign, or main astrology sign, is determined by where the sun was in the sky when you were born. Here are the twelve signs and the qualities of Light and Shadow that they embody.

Aries (March 21–April 20)
Light: courageous, fun, sincere
Shadow: impulsive, arrogant, stubborn

Taurus (April 21–May 20)
Light: loyal, patient, strong
Shadow: stubborn, lazy, possessive

Gemini (May 21–June 20)
Light: curious, versatile, charming
Shadow: inconsistent, superficial, anxious

Cancer (June 21–July 20)
Light: funny, loving, expressive
Shadow: moody, pessimistic, suspicious

Leo (July 21–August 21)
Light: kind, confident, loyal
Shadow: dominating, impatient, egotistical

Virgo (August 22–September 22)
Light: trustworthy, intelligent, analytical
Shadow: overly critical, judgmental, harsh

Libra (September 23–October 22)
Light: diplomatic, charming, fair
Shadow: superficial, detached, indecisive

Scorpio (October 23–November 22)
Light: intuitive, passionate, ambitious
Shadow: jealous, secretive, resentful

Sagittarius (November 23–December 20)
Light: optimistic, enthusiastic, gregarious
Shadow: blunt, careless, impatient

Capricorn (December 21–January 19)
Light: hardworking, ambitious, willful
Shadow: pessimistic, rigid, shy

Aquarius (January 20–February 18)
Light: adventurous, free-spirited, original
Shadow: unpredictable, detached, extremist

Pisces (February 19–March 20)
Light: intuitive, kind, creative
Shadow: escapist, delusional, overly sensitive

You also have a moon sign and a rising sign—which make up your unique inclinations. Moon signs are often said to represent how you feel internally, and rising signs represent how you appear to others on the outside. You can look these up if you know your birth time and location; do this either online or through an astrologer.

*L*et's explore your ego (sense of self). Using your sun sign as a starting point, write down the qualities you identify with in two lists: one for your *Light* self (the positive aspects of yourself that are out in the open) and one for your *Shadow* self (the negative aspects of yourself that are hidden in the dark, that bring a stab of negative feeling when you admit them). Give that Shadow aspect more love and compassion; it's a trait of yours that's been pushed to the extreme because it was deemed shameful or undesirable from an early age. Now, try looking at the qualities of your Shadow self with new eyes, and maybe begin to see them as positives—how they are teaching you. For example, people who are stubborn may also trust their own intuition.

LIGHT	SHADOW
_____	_____
_____	_____
_____	_____
_____	_____
_____	_____
_____	_____
_____	_____
_____	_____

LIGHT

SHADOW

LIGHT	SHADOW

LIGHT

SHADOW

_____ _____
_____ _____
_____ _____
_____ _____
_____ _____
_____ _____
_____ _____
_____ _____
_____ _____
_____ _____
_____ _____
_____ _____
_____ _____
_____ _____
_____ _____
_____ _____
_____ _____
_____ _____
_____ _____
_____ _____
_____ _____

LIGHT	SHADOW

LIGHT

SHADOW

Hecate

HOW TO BUILD AN ALTAR

The enchantress goddess of magic and crossroads, Hecate symbolizes the practice of worship as a deeply personal journey into your divine feminine. This is about turning inward and activating your intuition, while utilizing the wisdom of many cultures of our past to help support this practice. The only way out of the darkness is through it—and it can only help to have key goddesses support you with their wisdom and love. Hecate is a popular patron goddess because she is also the goddess of birth, death, and regeneration—all points where magic lives. Choose a patron goddess whom you connect with at this point in your journey. This journal is about helping you face the Shadow aspects of yourself that may be blocking you from what you truly want; but once you own them and realize what is at the root of your emotional triggers and causing your negative emotions (like anxiety, stress, depression, etc.), you are freed. Like the goddesses who have completed their journeys, you become nurturing, generous, loving, kind, wise, open, courageous, and grounded.

With that in mind,
let's talk about building an altar.

For the sake of this exercise, we're talking specifically about building an altar in your home or personal space. It's about creating a place you can retreat to when you need support and time for yourself or to connect with the universal energy (including all your goddesses, gods, spirit guides, angels, and loved ones—whatever you serve and what supports you). This is a physical safe space that serves as a portal between you and the metaphysical. Sometimes, it's a place where you can connect to or embody the goddess you're working with.

It's really simple to build an altar. Pick a space that is meaningful to you—this can represent an aspect of your life you're trying to call in (for example, build an altar on your desk to find greater business success or on your nightstand to bring in a romantic partner), or be a place where you like to meditate, journal, pull tarot cards, etc. This is where you will bring in magic, healing, and power, so make it meaningful to you. You may want to think about placing an altar inside a small cabinet that has doors, so you can shut the energy off for a while if you're feeling too activated by it.

If you choose a specific patron goddess, you can build your altar around her symbols—using fabrics in her favorite colors, cards or small statues of her physical depiction, little bronze representations of her animals, crystals connected to her spirit, or candles in her sacred colors. You may also change out fresh flowers as offerings when you do your ritual communion with your goddess—a time when you can recite an invocation (many are available online) or speak directly with her through meditation or prayer. Light the candles whenever you want to connect with the divine feminine; this can be done at specific times that are sacred to the goddess to be especially meaningful. For example, a ritual to Hecate should be done during a new moon (for Artemis, a nascent moon; for Demeter, a full moon). The altar can be as simple as a totem (card, picture, statue) of your goddess and a candle, and as complicated as a full mantel decked out in crystal grids (arrangements of healing crystals in specific formations that combine and expand their energy in a focused way). Do what feels good to you, and what you're able to act on now.

Alternately, you can create an altar that's more personally focused—a place to put the things you love or represent things you want to bring into your life: symbolic crystals for their metaphysical properties, your favorite incense to burn, essential oils to diffuse, statues of deities including goddesses and their associated relations (e.g., Ganesha, remover of obstacles and son of Parvati), or tarot cards that resonate with you. A good place to start is with a white candle and symbols of the four elemental energies: Earth/North (crystals, salt, bowl of sand, clay objects), Fire/South (candles, oils), Air/East (incense, feathers), and Water/West (a small bowl filled with water, seashells, river stones). Arrange the objects around the candle so that North is above, and the rest fall into place. Include a mirror if you'd like; it's a symbol of centering ourselves and finding the divine within. Smudge your altar often (with sage or palo santo) to protect your sacred space and draw in positive energies only.

Altars are an incredible opportunity for you to focus and create a visual representation of what you love and honor. It's also a sacred portal to connect with the universal energy we're all a part of. There are so many ways to explore building an altar; research whatever interests you and follow your intuition on this one.

List things that are meaningful to you as symbols right now…

Kali

EMBRACING YOUR SHADOW AND FACING YOUR FEARS

We all have a Shadow aspect of our personality, first identified in Carl Jung's psychoanalytic writings. Goddess energy *is* the yin, the darkness, the Shadow—and accepting and empowering that aspect of yourself will set you free from your fears, which hold you back from your greatness. The goddess Kali is the physical embodiment of the goddess Parvati's Shadow; she is the darkness that's split from Parvati's Lightness, and she is all destruction and chaos, blood and guts. Her tongue is often portrayed sticking out—which lends an air of playfulness and mocking to the seriousness in which we all fear our Shadows. But if we embrace the goddess Kali, and the dark side of ourselves, then we can be truly protected, safe, and liberated.

What you don't own, owns you.

We have to be fully balanced in embracing both our masculine *and* feminine sides in order to be our most whole, authentic selves. It's only from this grounded place of being balanced in Light and Shadow that we can really feel our power. By owning your darkness, you release your wounded ego and hurt self so that they can be healed and accepted by you. When you accept what's in your Shadow, these aspects won't be easily provoked or aggravated by others. And when our internal worlds become strong and balanced, we become beautiful beams of light that can create and attract everything we want.

Why is it important to own your Shadow? Our negative aspects are here to teach us and show us how to live in our true Light. If you don't own and understand the things you fear because you're so busy trying to deny them, you will keep attracting people and experiences you don't want into your life. You have to face and accept what you've hidden in your Shadow in order to grow. As the writer Florence Scovel Shinn said, "No man is your enemy, no man is your friend, everyone is your teacher."

Practice owning
your shadow.

To own your Shadow, you have to first recognize it in yourself. When we are triggered by someone or something, it usually means it's provoking our hidden aspects of self.

1. **Identify it.** Think back to a person or event in your life that has triggered negative emotions. Whittle down what aspect of that moment activated your negative reaction. Boil it down to one word or phrase. For example, did it tap into your fear that you're *unlovable*, *not good enough*, *jealous*, *selfish*, *controlling*, *demanding*, *undeserving*, *insignificant*, *ugly*, *stupid*, *weak*, etc.?

_____

_____

_____

_____

_____

_____

2. Understand that we all embody the spectrum of human traits—and that we are not defined by any one of them. Take these blocks that were likely created earlier in your life (being shamed by parents, teachers, or peers, or witnessing someone else being shamed for something), then *let go of the fear of it*. These traits are not definitive of who we are—we are the whole picture, the entire range of polarities in qualities. That is our humanity. So integrate these aspects you fear in yourself by speaking them into words in front of a mirror. Look at yourself in the mirror and say, "I am ____" until the words have no more meaning to you. Until you can laugh at yourself because you realize you can and may have been all these things, or could be under certain circumstances, but are not defined only by those words. You're not afraid of hearing the words anymore; they do not hold power. Remember: our perceived negative traits are here to teach and show us what we're here to learn and grow in; they hold us back when we deny or hide them. When you own that aspect, you can start to understand what it's trying to teach you about yourself.

3. **Write whatever is triggering you an angry letter.** If you feel stuck with an undesirable and intense unresolved emotion created by a person or experience, write it out in this journal. Pen a letter to who is making you so angry—was it something your mother said to you that activated your fear of being unimportant, selfish, stupid, etc.? What would you say to her in rebuttal? Release it through writing as fast as you can, saying everything you'd want to say to her face. This is for your eyes only, so feel very free here. Writing is a healthy way to release your intense and possibly toxic emotions—keep writing even if it gets harder, and at some point you may feel the pressure release around the triggering words. You may even help unearth what aspects of yourself that the person and experience is digging into, seeing from a fresh perspective what your ego is projecting. Then you can start to own it and unravel the stigma around it. The point is to release the intense grasp your ego is using to shove these aspects down in your Shadow.

_____

_____

_____

_____

4. **Love it.** Sit by yourself and place your hand over your heart. Breathe in and exhale as deeply as you can, and meditate on the negative feelings from a wider perspective. Where did they come from? Is there a specific memory or moment in your life that threw these aspects into your Shadow? For example, did you have an experience as a child—perhaps being shamed by a caregiver for wanting to keep your prized toy safe from other children—and then you threw the aspect of "I am selfish" into your Shadow? Call up that self, and hold that version of you in your mind's eye. Give it all the emotions it needs to heal—e.g., "You are generous *and* selfish. You deserve to care for and protect things that matter to you. You can be any of these things in any given situation, and that is okay. You are a whole, complex, beautiful human. You are not unworthy because of that. You are worthy because you are." Write out what you experience in this meditation here.

_____

_____

_____

_____

_____

rite down a current situation or person that's causing friction in your life. What aspect of this is really provoking you? What's at the root of the intense emotions you're feeling? Are you not being seen, not being respected, etc.? Why does that bother you? Try to get really specific and link it to a memory or experience you've had before, and where that fear may have been created and hidden in your Shadow.

Now, is that aspect true? How can you validate that denied aspect for yourself? A healthy Shadow is one that doesn't need external validation. A truly balanced divine feminine is confident, loving, generous, powerful, vulnerable, and supportive. Put this aspect through the practice above, and own yourself.

Yemoja

The beautiful moon, that physical representation of our wild feminine, has long captured the hearts and imaginations of human cultures. Many goddesses are associated with the moon, since it represents a constantly changing aspect of nature. Yoruba orisha Yemoja, goddess of the living waters (which are heavily influenced by the gravity of the moon), is a perfect divine spirit to connect with over moon rituals as she's deeply

connected with the crescent moon and all matters of the feminine. The moon goes through an entire cycle of birth and death thirteen times a year—while the sun, a representation of our masculine selves, does only one cycle a year. We're especially affected by the moon when we tap into our yin side, and when we sync our lives with the cycle of the moon, it's like riding the energetic wave of the universe: everything you're doing just comes easier. Each moon has unique vibrations as it moves into a different place in the solar system, entering a new astrology sign that can affect other factors of your experience during this specific moon's cycle.

Just a reminder that we are all made of interconnected stardust.

Moon Phases

You can tap into the moon's energy for your own growth and development. Here are the main cycles and rituals:

New Moon

A time for new beginnings! Best time to write down all the things you want to call into your life or make happen (manifest) on a list, meditate to open up your heart to receiving, and do a ritual to honor yourself and your commitments to the things you want to see in the next six months. Also a great time to tend to self-care rituals, such as taking an Epsom-salt bath, meditating, or journaling. It's a contemplative time of death and rebirth, where you'll want to evaluate where you're standing, what you've learned in the past six months, and what you're ready to let go of. Also known as the Crone phase of the goddess cycle, the new moon allows us to deepen our intuition and inner wisdom as we step into a new cycle.

Waxing Crescent

A time to start expanding your world and exploring possibilities to make the things on your list happen. Meet new people, say yes to new experiences, read, and follow your curiosities.

First Quarter Moon

Decision-making time. Often you'll find yourself at a crossroads, and this is the best time to commit to a path toward your goals. It's a great time to put yourself out there and get social. This first quarter moon time is also known as the Maiden phase, where you feel hopeful and excited about stepping out into the world, which makes decision-making feel less clouded by fear or anxiety. The best way to harness this moon phase's energy is to ride it like a wave carrying you easily toward your dreams.

Waxing Gibbous

A time for refining those decisions and intentions. You've gathered new information and experiences; now it's time to process them.

Full Moon

A time for release. A time for celebrating what you've harvested, or just general social vibes. Under the light of the full moon, we feel energized, and emotions tend to run high. Stay grounded by channeling that energy through socializing, connecting, and indulging in sensual pleasures. This is the Mother phase, where we feel fully seated and confident within our own femininity, and can be open to encouraging and nurturing others around us through connection.

A great time to perform a community ritual to call in a blessing from a goddess like Yemoja. Rituals for her can be done waterside, by tossing seven white roses or flowers into the water while also offering seven cowries (which represent wealth) and praying for the blessing you'd like to receive. You could also build an altar with a blue or white candle (Yemoja's colors) and offerings such as roses, cowries, crystals, and sweets (such as brown sugar, molasses, or fruit). Pray over it either in a moon circle or on your own—whatever feels good to you. It's also a good time to let go and forgive.

Waning Gibbous
A time for gratitude, relaxing, and regrouping.

Third Quarter
A time for reevaluating and trusting the universe. You may feel especially tired during this time, so you may want to turn inward and turn down more social obligations, focusing on your internal self and what you've learned recently. This is the Enchantress phase, a time to integrate what we've learned in this cycle (or over several cycles) into our lives.

Waning Crescent
A time for surrender and release. Let the universe unfold before you.

Rhiannon

GODDESSES AND CRYSTALS

Crystals have long served as a powerful connection between universal energy and humans, and they can be wonderful enhancements to your goddess practice. Rhiannon, a powerful Welsh goddess and fairy princess, draws her power from her connection with nature. She's a goddess who can manifest anything she desires, especially when she's working in connection with the earth—and you can wield some of that magic for yourself when working with crystals. Before we get specific, here are the five stones everyone should have in their bag: crystal quartz (powerful amplifier), amethyst (protection and attracts calm, positive energy), black tourmaline (absorbs negativity, gives protection), smoky quartz (grounding, de-stressing), and citrine (attracts abundance, success, and positivity).

Crystal Magic

Here's a list of crystals that are associated with specific goddesses; this may be helpful if you're building an altar or performing rituals or meditations to commune with your goddess, as they vibrate on the same energetic planes as their corresponding goddess. While not strictly prescriptive, these stones may help deepen your connections—and you know that goddesses are attracted to all things of beauty and nature.

Aditi (Hindu mother goddess of the infinite universe): blue topaz

Amaterasu (Shinto goddess of the sun): pyrite, topaz

Aphrodite (Greek goddess of love): rose quartz

Artemis (Greek goddess of the hunt, wilderness, and the moon): dendrite, amethyst

Athena (Greek goddess of wisdom, arts, and war): citrine, carnelian, pyrite

Bast (Egyptian goddess of sex, magic, and pleasure): tiger's-eye

Brigit (Irish goddess of creative arts and healing): green quartz

Chalchiuhtlicue (Aztec goddess of waters and reinvention): jade

Demeter (Greek goddess of abundance): citrine

Estsanatlehi (Native American goddess of sky and earth): turquoise

Freya (Norse goddess of love): cat's-eye, amber

Gaia (Greek goddess of the earth): agate, smoky quartz

Hathor (Egyptian goddess of love and joy): malachite, turquoise

Hecate (Greek goddess of magic and crossroads): jet, labradorite

Isis (Egyptian goddess of magic): carnelian, desert rose

Ixchel (Mayan goddess of creativity, water, fertility, and fate): opal

Kuan Yin (Chinese goddess of mercy and compassion): jade, aventurine, pearl

Oshun (Yoruba goddess of sweet waters, love, beauty, and creation): amber, coral

Pele (Hawai'ian goddess of fire): obsidian

Rhiannon (Welsh goddess of protection): moonstone, bloodstone

Tara (Hindu goddess of compassion and protection): aventurine, jade

Gaia

HEALING THROUGH NATURE AND GRATITUDE

Gaia is the mother earth goddess who created all living things and provides for us through the abundance of the earth. She is the prototypical mother goddess, and through her we can always heal and grow. There are studies that show connecting with nature is super powerful for our health, and going out to nature to connect with Gaia can be an important practice for grounding us in our busy, noisy lives. She is the living energy of renewal, cycles, seasons, and healing.

Gratitude is also an important part of respecting and connecting with Gaia—and with ourselves. Studies have shown that a practice of gratitude improves our ability to be resilient and optimistic and, in turn, happier in our everyday lives. When we practice gratitude, we are invoking Gaia, thanking her for all the abundance she provides, and appreciating the good in our lives.

Connecting with Gaia

It's simple to connect with Gaia: just go outside. Find a place in nature that makes you feel good—the beach, a park, the forest, a trail, the desert. Sit on the earth (be it sandy beach or grassy field), and close your eyes. Say a little invocation to call out Gaia; let this be personal to you. (Following is a translated Homeric invocation for you to start.) Then, as you focus on inhaling and exhaling, imagine a golden light coming through your body from the earth. The light fills your body, from your root chakra (at the base of your spine, see also: Parvati) up to the tips of your ears. Feel a warm, nurturing energy from that light come over you. Fill your heart. Send out gratitude. When you feel finished, say a closing note of thanks to Gaia and open your eyes. Celebrate and seal your prayer with treats made with honey or barley, which are ancient traditional offerings to Gaia.

Of her I sing, the All-Mother
old and rock-hard and beautiful.

Of her I sing, the nourisher,
she upon whom everything feeds.
Of Gaia I sing. Whoever you are,
wherever you are, she feeds you

from her sacred treasury of life.
Bountiful harvests, beautiful

Children, the fullness of life:
these are her gifts. Praise her.

—HOMERIC HYMN TO GAIA

*E*very morning, make a list of three things that you're grateful for. There's nothing too small or too large; everything counts. You may connect with Gaia further by lighting a candle (green, blue, or white) to invoke her spirit, by writing at your altar, or by sitting in front of an open window so that fresh, earthy air can come in. Keep it simple so that it's something you can do every day; challenge yourself to see how many days in a row you can do this, and watch the feeling of abundance and optimism start to fill up in you.

Creiddylad

HOW TO SELF-CARE LIKE A GODDESS

The Welsh goddess of flowers and spring, Creiddylad teaches us the importance of self-care. Through her mythology, we learn that as seasons change and time passes, we are the only constant. It is through taking care of ourselves, filling up our own wells, and putting our own health first that we're able to keep an eternal spring within us, the way Creiddylad does. Taking time for yourself cultivates self-respect, self-love, and vibrant energy—so you may shine as brilliant as a goddess and bring joy everywhere you go. Also, turning inward and focusing on how you're feeling is very in line with the *yin* energy that we're tapping into here—your self-care is breaking down the barriers of patriarchy. So it is not only your indulgence, but also your duty to take care of yourself!

Here are seven self-care rituals
to make you feel aligned
with your inner goddess.

1. Bring flowers into your home. Nature expresses joy in flowers, and bringing in these beautiful symbols of nature's abundance and power will make your heart feel full. Whether you buy yourself a bouquet or pluck a single bloom from your yard, bringing nature into your home will make you feel better. Not into flowers? Try bringing in house plants! They will help purify the air *and* give you the benefit of that nature bomb of happiness.

2. Take a bath. Use Epsom salts to help pull out the toxins in your body. Light candles, drop in petals from your flowers as they're on their way out, hang a eucalyptus branch, or add drops of your favorite essential oils. Add a clay or sheet mask. Take twenty minutes of peace; feel your inner glow come out.

3. **Do restorative yoga.** At home with an online video or out at a studio class, take the time to stretch out and really get in touch with your body.

4. **Take a walk in nature.** Even dare to plant your feet barefoot in the earth, and let it soak up all that powerful healing energy.

5. **Meditate with crystals.** Find ones that vibe with the goddess or energy you want to connect with, and spend some time in quiet meditation. Look up grids that you can create around you to call in certain vibrations, or practice opening up your chakras (see: Parvati).

6. **Try an Abhyanga self-massage.** An ancient Ayurvedic technique for calming your system, it uses oils such as almond, coconut, or safflower depending on your *dosha*, or body type (you can find yours by taking an online quiz or visiting an Ayurvedic practitioner), to give yourself a massage from scalp to toes that takes

about fifteen to twenty minutes. Extremely beneficial for relaxing your nervous system and bringing you back into your body.

7. Journal out your affirmations. Give yourself credit for what you're proud of accomplishing lately, however small or large. It's all these small steps that add up to big changes, and taking the time to recognize them is a way to honor yourself and your work.

_____

_____

_____

_____

_____

_____

_____

_____

_____

*M*ake a list of ways you like to practice self-care. This can be things you already do, or things you'd like to try; it's just nice to keep a list of things that make you feel good to reference if you're feeling especially frazzled. More examples include: doing nothing, reading, lying down and quietly inhaling through one nostril and out the other by pressing down one side with your finger and alternating, taking a catnap in the sun, taking the time to put on makeup, putting on all your favorite jewelry; the possibilities are endless. It's about taking the time—from a one-minute swipe of lipstick to a twenty-minute self-massage to an hour-long nap—to be with yourself, and do something *for* you, that makes *you* feel good. No other purpose.

Aphrodite

CALLING IN LOVE

The Greek goddess of love and beauty, Aphrodite, is the one to call on when you want romance to blossom in your life—whether you're seeking love from a partner, a deeper self-love, or more passion in your life in general. Aphrodite is the goddess of passion and attraction, the initial excitement you feel for things—so call on her when you're looking to wake up your zeal for life, especially in the heart department. She's an incredibly powerful goddess, capricious and flirtatious, and opens up that aspect of yourself—but she is not necessarily a goddess of lasting partnerships or stable commitment, so keep that in mind as you work with her.

Rituals to commune with Aphrodite:

1. Dance. Even if it's in your own room, in your own style, to the tune in your own head—one of the greatest ways Aphrodite moves through us is in dance.

2. Build a beautiful altar to her. This is a goddess who *loves* beauty and being adored. Use flowers, scents like cinnamon and myrrh, luxurious silks, pearls, and glittering golden objects. Her favorite fruits are pomegranate and apple. She loves milk and honey. Follow your intuition and creativity on how to represent these offerings in your altar to her.

3. Buy yourself flowers as an offering to her and to your inner goddess. Red roses are her most favored flower—representing the heart and passion—but she also loves poppies, anemones, lilies, myrtle, crocus, and narcissus. Always use fresh flowers to honor her.

4. Place objects in your bedroom that represent her favorite animals: swans, geese, and ducks. Often, these appear in pairs—and having pairs attracts a partnership into your life.

5. Take a bath. Scent the water with luxurious oils such as rose, cinnamon, and myrrh; sprinkle in rose petals; and surround yourself with candles and your favorite music. Romance yourself. This is the goddess to channel for self-care and tapping into your own sexuality.

6. Meditate with rose quartz. This stone allows you to tap into the love vibration, which is also the channel that passionate and playful Aphrodite works on.

The most important message you can get from Aphrodite is to be so in love with your own life and yourself that you can't help but feel the love spill into all aspects of your life. You are the one you're waiting for—and when you truly accept and love yourself, the romance you're looking for just may appear.

Write a list of ways you like to honor yourself and show yourself love. Write ways that others make you feel loved and how you show love toward others. Write down memories, moments, and experiences that have made you feel irresistible—the things that give you a burst of excitement in your gut and a tingle in your spine.

Athena

The Greek goddess of wisdom, Athena, is the one to invoke when you're embarking on a creative endeavor or pursuing goals. Also a strategic goddess of war, Athena offers counsel to mortals on the best defensive strategies—and she is a patron goddess of many crafts, including writing, weaving, and the arts. You can call on Athena's assistance by setting up an altar for her in your creative space—with an image of her (which you can even make yourself, in the true spirit of the goddess of craftsmanship); symbols of her familiars (the snake or the owl); or a crystal (citrine, carnelian, and pyrite would be especially good).

rite down your goals for the next year. If you like candles, light one in gold, yellow, or green—Athena's chosen colors—in your altar while you make your list and every time you work on your goals. However small or big, trivial or meaningful, get all those dreams out there. Include personal and professional targets.

YEAR

_____

_____

_____

_____

_____

_____

_____

_____

_____

_____

_____

_____

hen write down your objectives for the next month. Again, nothing is too small or too big. This is a great opportunity to break your year-long plans into smaller steps that you'll work toward each month.

MONTH

*A*t the beginning of every week, write down your goals for the next seven days. Personal (hang out with at least one friend during the week), physical (go to the gym three times), and professional (ask for that raise!).

WEEK

*n*ow here's where the magic happens. Make a habit of writing down your goals every night for a month. Every. Single. Night. Writing down your intentions before you go to bed engages your subconscious to help you problem solve and work toward those objectives while you're in a restorative sleep mode. Write down whatever you want to achieve—whether it be a major dream that comes to mind, or a to-do list for the next day. Just write it down. The practice of writing already puts all these dreams into action. You might wake up with solutions to problems you've been trying to crack, ideas for new ways to pursue your goals, and an overall sense of positivity and power.

When working with Athena, you want her assistance in being strategic and steadfast in pursuit of your goals and calling in all the things you'd like to manifest for your life. Discipline matters more than motivation, and when working with this goddess of wisdom—you'll experience it in motion. Try this simple practice of writing down your goals—and see how far you'll be in a year. You may just surprise yourself.

DAILY

DAILY

DAILY

DAILY

DAILY

DAILY

DAILY

BUILDING BOUNDARIES

The Hindu goddess of removing obstacles, Durga is the divinity to invoke when you're going through difficult challenges. Invoke the protective spirit of Durga to help you develop better personal boundaries and therefore manage the expectations and emotions that come from outside experiences.

First: take inventory. What is happening outside of you that you are feeling personally? What is out of your control but triggering you anyway? Have people asked too much of you, or more than you're willing to give, but you have a hard time saying no? Why is that? Are there times you feel hurt but can't speak up? Journal these answers.

Then: reevaluate what's important to you. Setting strong boundaries is a form of self-care. We all have limited time and space on this earth, and even more so when we feel the need to give simply because we are asked. People will always test your boundaries, and you have to strengthen your boundaries and protect your sacred inner space. Write down what you value: e.g., time alone, saying no, opportunities you'd like to attract, people who matter to you, important activities, things you enjoy, goals you've set for yourself, etiquette and manners that are meaningful to you, personal values. When you know what is most important to you, then you won't give in so easily to everyone else's demands.

inally: sit with your spine straight and close your eyes. Visualize a circle forming around you. Bring in symbols of things that make you feel safe. Open up the circle to enclose those objects. Then bring in symbols of things that make you feel nurtured and loved—be it plants, flowers, animals, or objects, but *not* other people. Let this space be just for you. Allow your circle of protection to expand a bit more to include all these things you love. Finally, visually enforce your circle so that you can see a strong vibration coming from it. Channel Durga to help you pour your energy and heart into your circle, and feel the sensation of calm, happy safety come over you in your bubble. Then say a short prayer of gratitude to Durga, and open your eyes.

Keep Growing

Review and reevaluate the values you wrote down often. You're allowed to grow and change your mind, challenge old beliefs, and shed the things that don't work for you. When you know your values, you are able to speak them—and that's where authenticity lives. When you believe one thing and do/say another, your character suffers. When you're in an uncomfortable position, use that as an opportunity to once again examine why it violated your boundaries (maybe it's time to set up new ones or to reexamine what's in your Shadow), so that you can accept and love all aspects of yourself wholeheartedly.

Xochiquetzal

FLOWERS AS SYMBOLISM

It was common in the Victorian era for flower bouquets to read as secret messages from sender to recipient—but this practice goes back so much further, as many goddesses are associated with various flowers. Xochiquetzal is symbolized by the marigolds whose feather-like petals are a direct translation of her name and thus carry the spirit of her blessings. Worshippers of Xochiquetzal channel her essence by wearing marigolds, decorating altars, and using marigolds to honor their deceased.

Besides their beauty and color, flowers represent the cycle of life and the fertility of plants and nature in general—as women and the divine feminine do. So bring flowers into your goddess practice, whether

placing offerings at your altar, adorning your nightstand with two roses to bring in the energy of a partner, or displaying positive sunflowers in your kitchen. Flowers can work on both the levels of self-care and symbolism for the energy you want to attract from the universe and the goddesses you want to honor.

Goddess Flowers

Here's a list of goddesses, their areas of influence, and their corresponding flowers to start your rituals:

Aphrodite (passionate love, self-care, indulgence): rose, anemone, poppy, myrtle

Bast (protection, good health): cattail, reed, mint

Benten (good fortune, flow): lotus, water lily, yellow flowers

Brigit (wisdom, fertility, healing): dandelion, snowdrop, shamrock

Creiddylad (self-preservation, love, rebirth): holly, ivy, mayflower

Demeter (abundance, generosity): poppy, sunflower, foxglove, daisy, columbine

Freya (courage): rose, tansy

Hathor (healing, regeneration): blue lotus

Hecate (reinvention, witchcraft, protection): night-blooming flowers (e.g., evening primrose, moonflower, cereus)

Kuan Yin (compassion, mercy): white lotus, willow branch, white flowers

Laka (dance, love, joy): maile, hala pepe, 'ie 'ie, ki, palai

Lakshmi (love, light): lotus

Mazu (courage, compassion): peach blossom, lotus, peony

Oshun (healing heartbreak, forgiveness): sunflower

Pele (power, passion): ohia lehua

Psyche (spirituality, healing): lily of the valley, sweet alyssum, water lily

Rhiannon (magic, overcoming, manifesting): narcissus, daffodil, pansy, forsythia

Yemoja (protection, mothering): white rose

Xochiquetzal (creativity, love, death, sexuality): marigold, rose

B uy yourself flowers. Whatever you're drawn to—and see what they might symbolize. Make an arrangement symbolizing different things you want to call in.

or

D raw your favorite or most meaningful flowers in the following pages. Flowers are not always available or accessible, but visual representations work just as well for calling in that energy. Don't worry about skill level—just get out your favorite creative tools and have fun with it. That truly channels the fun-loving and creative spirit of Xochiquetzal.

Isis

HOW TO HEAL A BROKEN HEART

Isis, the Egyptian goddess of magic, helps guide us on a journey through grief—illustrated in her own journey. She feels our intense grief as we go through loss and heartache, and she ushers us on a journey to search for our wholeness again. Finally, she's there for us as we find ourselves coming out the other side. While grief never leaves us, it does change shape within us. Call on Isis for the strength to persevere and carry on.

The Healing Process

Isis teaches us that first we must grieve our loss—an intense period of emotion that can manifest in many different ways. Practice extreme self-compassion during this time, and do what you need to do to feel comfortable and safe. Writing in a journal during this time could be helpful, scribbling out your raw emotions when you may struggle to find the words to express to someone else. There's no judgment here in these pages. Seek professional help if you need; this can be one of the greatest gifts you give yourself: a trained, objective specialist to help you carry this load.

Then, when you're ready to move into the next phase, you may find yourself searching for what will fill the hole that the loss has created. Be patient with yourself. Take it one day at a time, and focus on things—however small—that make you happy. This might be a good time to start a gratitude practice (see: Gaia), or to reflect on lessons you learned through the experience. For example: What did you want that you were not receiving in that relationship or job? Or what did you take for granted that you can now appreciate fully?

*n*ow make a list of what you *do* want. Include every detail of each thing you want—e.g., when manifesting a new job, write down what you want from that job: a certain salary, position, environment, location, etc. This will be a time where opportunities will come along to test you. The universe wants us to be happy and whole, aligned with our life's calling and journey—and that can only happen when we stop settling for anything but what our souls truly want. A job opportunity comes, but doesn't make your heart sing? A date happens, but you didn't feel anything? Let it pass. Use it as an opportunity to learn more about what you do want or reflect on any patterns that you might be trapped in. These patterns are reflections of what we witnessed and were modeled for us in our childhoods; some of the patterns are unhealthy and hold us back from getting what we want. We may be trapped in a shame-and-pain cycle within our Shadow (see: Kali). If we keep settling for things that are just okay, instead of striving toward the full experience of what's calling us, then we hold ourselves down. We have to learn the lessons of what patterns we're trapped in to break out of these cycles and evolve into our next level.

When you move through life's phases, also be on a lookout for signs from the universe. Something several friends mention to you, an article you read, an image you see that stirs you—pay attention to these. Signs often come in threes. Keep holding to your standards and working toward your goals, trusting that, with time, the space in your heart will change shape. And then, without much pomp or circumstance, you might just find that one day it does change. If you try something new, go somewhere new, meet someone new—you might find that opportunities you've always dreamed of will start showing up. Through Isis, we learn that true healing comes from accepting that something bigger and better is still coming for us—that the loss will not define our lives. It may shape your life, but you will be a sum of everything in this divine journey.

Amaterasu

SHINING THE LIGHT WITHIN

The Shinto sun goddess Amaterasu is a divinity who helps us find the Light within ourselves. In her myth, she retreats to a dark cave after being harassed by her brother Susano-o. She's lured out of self-exile after catching a glance of herself in a mirror, astonished by her own beauty and brilliance. Her story tells us to defeat those who cause us stress or harm by finding our own inner Light—and, just like the sun, letting it shine from within us to warm ourselves and everything around us. It is with our own inner strength, positivity, and courage that we're able to heal ourselves. There are traditional festivals to honor Amaterasu every year on the equinoxes (around March 21 and September 21), which celebrate the perfect balance between light and dark, and on the solstices (around June 21 and December 21), to toast the ever-renewing cycle of light and dark. Perform a ritual to invoke Amaterasu when you're especially stressed and feeling trapped in darkness—call on her to restore your faith and light the way.

ere's a simple ritual for calling in Amaterasu. First you need a mirror, since that is her major symbol (in fact, her original mirror is said to be stored in a shrine in central Japan, where they move it every twenty years within a circuit of holy shrines to celebrate and honor the goddess). This can be a special mirror that you dedicate for this purpose (you can do this by cleaning a new mirror with sun-soaked sake and saying a prayer to Amaterasu to bless this special object), or it can simply be your bathroom mirror. You can make an altar or a special space for this meditation by using fresh flowers in yellow or gold, jade crystals, and magatama beads (a man-made, decorative jewel that is often used in Japanese ceremonies).

Situate yourself in front of the mirror, place your palms in prayer position in front of your heart, and bow slightly to the mirror. Then fix your gaze on your reflection as you chant the goddess's name eight times (eight is the Shinto number of perfection, so this number will be especially appealing to Amaterasu) to bring yourself into a calm, meditative state. Breathe deeply and reflect on something that is upsetting you and why you're being triggered by it; think about what you're hiding in your Shadow that's rising up in you and creating negative emotions. What are you resisting? What are you putting off or fearing? Are there signs that keep popping up of things you keep meaning to explore? While we are not in control of what happens around us, we *are* in control of ourselves and how we allow outside circumstances to affect us. How can you use your own strength to reframe and overcome this obstacle? Are you facing a challenge because it's something you feel you should do, instead of what you want to do? Above all of the storm clouds of our lives is a perpetual sun and clear blue sky.

After five to ten minutes of this meditation (stop when it feels right), take a moment to inhale and close your eyes. Imagine warm, golden liquid sunshine filling your body from the top of your head all the way down to your toes. Then exhale and bow to the mirror to close your ritual.

Write down everything that came up for you in this practice here. Do it daily for a few days—preferably in the morning—and see what surfaces for you. It may take a while to break through these blockages, but this practice allows you to honor yourself and creates space for positive energy and your own Light to come through.

Parvati

OPENING YOUR CHAKRAS

Chakras are the energy centers of your body, derived from a Sanskrit word meaning "wheel" or "cycle." There are seven of them along our spine, with one above the crown of our head, that govern our energy. When a chakra is blocked or overactive, it can be a sign that an area of our life is under stress, and we act and feel out of sorts. There are many techniques for balancing the chakras, and when they're all aligned and open, your energy is a beautiful rainbow (representing true harmony and balance). Goddesses are also tied to these chakras, helping them flow through you when you get in touch with your divine feminine. For example, Parvati, the Hindu goddess of love and devotion, assists in opening up your heart chakra.

To get in touch with your chakras and open up your heart space, sit in a chair with your feet firmly planted on the ground. Close your eyes, and inhale deeply. With each inhale, imagine the chakra color coming up from the earth through your left leg, filling the chakra space, then returning down your right leg. Then take another breath, and reverse the movement. Do this until the color feels bright in your mind's eye; and then move onto the next chakra.

First/Root Chakra
Location: Base of your spine
Color: Red
Purpose: Grounding, safety, and security, especially in your body and in physical spaces outside your body. If you're feeling insecure or threatened, this chakra is blocked. If you're feeling too grounded and walled up, it may be overactive.
Goddess: Gaia, goddess of creation and earth.

Second/Sacral Chakra
Location: Above pelvis, between the hips
Color: Orange
Purpose: Emotions, creativity, sexuality. If you feel stiff or unemotional, this chakra is blocked. If you feel too emotional and attached, it's overactive.
Goddess: Aphrodite, goddess of love and sexuality

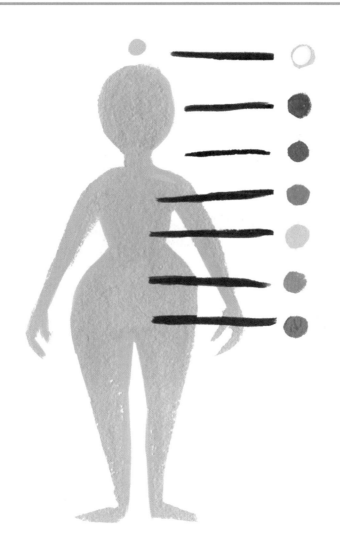

Third/Solar Plexus Chakra
Location: Solar plexus

Color: Yellow

Purpose: Personal power, self-confidence, will. If you feel passive and indecisive, this chakra is blocked. If you feel domineering and aggressive, it may be overactive.

Goddess: Athena, goddess of wisdom and personal power

Fourth/Heart Chakra
Location: Heart

Color: Green or pink

Purpose: Love and compassion. If you feel cold and distant, this chakra is blocked. If you feel desperate and possessive in love, then it may be overactive, and you need to redirect that energy to nurturing yourself.

Goddess: Parvati, goddess of love and devotion

Fifth/Throat Chakra
Location: Throat

Color: Blue

Purpose: Voice, self-expression, communication. If you feel misunderstood or can't find the right words, this chakra is blocked. If you're speaking too much and keep people at a distance, this may be overactive.

Goddess: Oya, goddess of the storms and winds—including your breath

Sixth/Third Eye Chakra

Location: Third eye, on your forehead, between the eyes

Color: Purple or indigo

Purpose: Intuition, vision, insight. If you're feeling very indecisive and relying too much on outside opinions to make decisions, this chakra could be blocked. If you're too lost in a world of your own daydreams, this chakra may be overactive.

Goddess: Hecate, goddess of magic and crossroads

Seventh/Crown Chakra

Location: Above the crown of the head

Color: White

Purpose: Connection with spirituality, tuned into the universe, wisdom. If you don't feel in tune with the universal energy, whatever you may call it, or are too narrow in your thinking, this aspect may be blocked. If you're intellectualizing too much and living in your head-space, this aspect may be overactive.

Goddess: Aditi, mother goddess of the endless universe

Additional practices to unblock chakras: yoga poses that open up specific chakra spaces; meditation with crystals of corresponding colors placed on blocked chakras; or a chakra clearing/energy healer (such as Reiki).